THE AUTHENTIC LEADER AS SERVANT (ALS)

ALS II COURSE 4
ENCOURAGEMENT LEADERSHIP
Attributes, Principles, and Practices

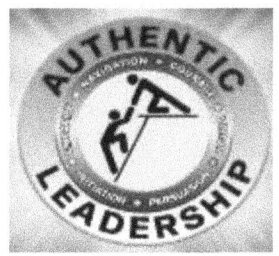

SYLVANUS N. WOSU, Ph.D

THE AUTHENTIC LEADER AS SERVANT
ALS II COURSE 4
Developing Encouragement Leadership Attributes, Principles, and Practices

© Copyright 2024 by Sylvanus N. Wosu Ph.D.

Printed in the United States of America
ISBN: 979-8-9868665-5-0

All rights reserved. No part of this book may be reproduced or transmitted in any form or by any means, electronic or mechanical, including photocopying, recording, or by any information storage and retrieval system, without permission in writing from the copyright owner.

Bible quotations are from the New King James (NKJV) version of the Bible unless otherwise indicated.

Other versions used in this book are the New International Version (NIV), New Living Translation (NLT), King James Version (KJV), English Standard Version (ESV), and Good News Translation (GNT). Unless otherwise specified, NKJV should be assumed.

The views expressed in this work are solely those of the author and do not necessarily reflect the views of the publisher, and the publisher disclaims any responsibility for them.

To order additional copies of this book, contact:
Proisle Publishing Services LLC
39-67 58th Street, 1st floor
Woodside, NY 11377, USA
Phone: (+1 646-480-0129)
info@proislepublishing.com

TABLE OF CONTENTS

FOREWORD	XI
ACKNOWLEDGMENTS	XV
DEDICATION	XVII
PREFACE	19
About Leader As Servant Leadership (LSL) Model	22
About the Authentic Leader as Servant (ALS)	25
About the ALS Courses	26

CHAPTER 1
UNDERSTANDING LEADERSHIP ATTRIBUTES   35

- Functional Definitions — 35
- Comparisons With Other Works — 40
- Principle of Leadership Attribute — 42
- Authentic Leadership Attributes — 43
- Summary 1 Understanding Leadership Process — 48

CHAPTER 2
ENCOURAGEMENT LEADERSHIP ATTRIBUTE   51

- Servant Leadership Encouragement Attribute — 52
- Principle of Leadership Encouragement Attribute — 53
- Summary 2 Encouragement Leadership Attribute — 56

CHAPTER 3
DEVELOPING ENCOURAGEMENT-AFFIRMATION   59

- Be Positive in Words and Actions — 59
- Be Personal and Purposeful in Words — 60
- Summary 3 Developing Encouragement-Affirmation — 61

CHAPTER 4
DEVELOPING ENCOURAGEMENT- EXALTATION   63

- Readiness to Exalt Followers' Performance — 63
- Authenticity and Capacity to Motivate — 64
- Summary 4 Developing Encouragement-Exaltation — 64

CHAPTER 5
DEVELOPING ENCOURAGEMENT-COMPASSION   67

- BE GENEROUS TO MEET THE NEEDS OF OTHERS — 67
- BE COURAGEOUS TO STAND BEHIND THE FOLLOWERS — 67

POSITIVE ATTITUDE AND COMMITMENT TO MENTOR 68
BRING COMFORT AND RELIEF IN CONSOLATION 69
ENGAGE IN RECONCILIATION TO BUILD RELATIONSHIPS 70
SUMMARY 5 DEVELOPING ENCOURAGEMENT–COMPASSION 71

TOPIC INDEX   75
REFERENCES   77

Foreword

The modern world today is obsessed with standardization and modalities. As a result, in the realm of leadership, many books have spout associated leadership theories and models and explain them as the path to follow. However, the critical dimensions that distinguish the effectiveness of any leadership process are the values and attribute the leader brings to the table; desired change is influenced by leadership styles or standards. These many standards and theories of leadership often are not in step with the changing times or the followers' needs. The trend is a bit like stocking different kinds of foods in a grocery store and expecting that they will meet everybody's needs the same way and at all times. Aisles are packed with varieties of food with expiration dates in the future, but getting the best deal on the products is what really matters to those who buy and use the products

In many ways, this is the state of leadership in the modern world. Increasingly, even leaders of public institutions are tasked with turning a profit for themselves or the organization they serve. The idea of a "leader" seems to float uneasily alongside the ranks of fundraisers or profit raisers in contrast to any kind of role model for followers or employees. That which is knowable, measurable, and marketable has surpassed the difficult intangibility of strong moral leadership attributes as the central guideline for achievement and success.

In this complicated space, Dr. Sylvanus Wosu introduces his complex idea of the Leader as a Servant Leadership, which is in this book, modeled on Christian tradition. Like all intricate ideas, Dr. Wosu's central point depends on a paradox: a person is best qualified to lead when he or she is most ready to serve. This paradox has been monopolized rhetorically by "public servants" who often serve either self-interest or the interests of specific lobbies. The Authentic Leader as Servant penetrates past the superficial concept of "serving" and details the internal state of true servitude or Servanthood.

While the book is primarily focused on the Christian model of leadership attributes such as discipleship, empathy, affection, and Servanthood, it does so not merely on the grounds of blind faith, but rather via numerous contemporary sociological and business-driven studies on how leaders should seek a leader-follower relationship that is simultaneously productive and nurturing. Dr. Wosu's most piercing insights always involve this secular–Christian dialogue. This book demonstrates that Christ's model for leadership is one that may exist successfully outside the confines of a faith relationship; it places the values of Christ's religious significance in leadership at the center of the framework. It is clear from Dr. Wosu's generous own life story of faith—a faith tested by humbling difficulties—is at the center of both his orientation and motivation for writing.

In language that is so concise, it is often illustrated in mathematical formulas; Dr. Wosu explains the deep structural integrity of Christ's Leader as the Servant Leadership model. One could imagine leaders of any doctrine benefiting from the analyses contained in these pages. The book's message repeatedly encourages the reader to imagine a scenario or reflect on memories and personal experiences to prove or test its many points. Thus, the book depends on a form of praxis, a lesson that could be or has been enacted, by the participating reader. I am very impressed at the volume and level of thinking of the author. Parts of the book involve his personal story, which is especially riveting. I cannot imagine what he had to endure, which he referred to as a" wilderness walk," to accomplish the goal he set for himself. His life stories on these pages are inspiring and stimulating.

In this way, the text eschews dogmatism in favor of the self-discovery Socratic Method of teaching and learning. The reader is not badgered into complying with a religious objective but is rather asked to consider the applicability of difficult biblical concepts in relation to modern life. It is a fascinating and very thought-provoking read.

Hence, the book does not seek to make the leader a servant, a cookie-cutter corporate buzzword, but rather asks the reader to imagine him or herself interacting with a range of concepts. One of Dr. Wosu's great strengths is his reservation when it comes to forcing his reading's interpretation on the material he presents.

The book parallels Biblical and modern leadership scenarios in ways that consistently provoke thought, and while it is clear Dr. Wosu has his particular leadership style; the space for the reader's own thoughts is always left open.

The book could not have been written in any other way with integrity. Its format and formulas are offered to the reader of the leader as a servant role that it analyzes in its pages. To find a text that instructs from this humble position is profoundly refreshing in a genre that is often packaged inside a cover with a sizeable picture of the "modest" author, smiling egotistically beneath a name spelled out in large, gold lettering. Throughout its pages, this text feels as if it serves the reader.

In the end, this is the most satisfying aspect of the book. There is no standardized approach to achieving successful leadership. There is no promise of power and a bigger payday; in fact, the book often proffers just the opposite. The reader is not encouraged to devalue the experience of leadership by finding some economic metric for marking success but is rather asked to think deeply about the most basic elements of internal and social interaction within the framework of a Christian tradition. What this means will be different for every reader. Indeed, even in the context of single chapters, I found myself questioning or re-evaluating moments of my own life. This book serves; it doesn't feel like filling in multiple-choice questions, staring at a wall of flavorless grocery products, or hearing the endless servant promises of today's political scene. It feels like a humble invitation to consider a single paradoxical element of a profoundly productive tradition.

-Tobias Bates

Acknowledgments

A book on leadership attributes as aspects of Servant Leadership sprouted from the wealth of knowledge and the inspirations of many other leaders. Their writings were sources of inspiration, challenges, and examples of excellence to emulate. I acknowledge the leaders listed below for their help in one way or the other. I am very grateful and I hereby express my appreciation and thanks:

Mr. Wayne Holt, introduced me first to the subject of Servanthood in one of our Stephen Ministerial Training classes, and he is the one who has conducted his life as a leader–servant; he encouraged me throughout my writing;

Dr. Harvey Borovetz, Distinguished Professor and Chair of the Bioengineering Department, is a leader-servant in many ways, he modeled Servanthood and encouragement attributes throughout his leadership in an academic setting.

Dr. Clifford and Dr. Patience Obih, in so many measures exemplified the practical leadership attributes discussed in this book.

Pastor Lance Lecocq, Lead Pastor of Monroeville Assembly of God, for his excellent model of servanthood, empowerment, and emulation attributes to the ministerial team, I am thankful for his motivation and encouragement throughout the several hours on this project;

To my administrative assistant, Ms. Terri Cook, who was always the first to review the manuscript; I am very grateful for her dedication.

To the African Christian Fellowship USA, institutions, and all other organizations where I have served in one leadership capacity or the other, thank you for affording me senior leadership positions that provided the leadership platform and opportunities to grow as a leader.

Dr. Lawrence Owoputi, a brother I am proud to call my friend; for his dedication to serving others, his generosity, healing care, and responsibility attributes during our term in office and in chapter leadership positions; he taught me that excellent following is also part of good leadership;

To Tobias Bates, for his editorial work on the original draft of the book, and his dedication to completing the work.

Mr. Edward F. Kondis, a member of our Engineering Board of Visitors, for his always encouraging and moral support;

Dr. Enefaa N. Wosu, my wife and life partner, for her love, commitment, and prayer support, especially during those long night hours I was not there for her and her constant reminder of who I must be as a leader-servant. Without her support, forbearance, wisdom, and encouragement, this project would not have been completed; I say, thank you very much.

And to God alone be all the glory and honor for the divine inspiration and guidance in initiating and completing this life-transforming book project.

Dedication

I humbly submit this book back unto the gracious hands of God who inspired the writings through His Holy Spirit!

I dedicate this book to my virtuous wife of 45 years, Rev. (Dr.) Enefaa Wosu whose spiritual leadership is an important gateway to our home, and to our four wonderful children—Prof. Eliada Wosu-Griffin EL, HeCareth, Tamuno-Emi, and Chidinma. From them all, I learnt what it meant to be a leader-servant. I could not be blessed with better teachers.

Preface

What characteristics did Biblical leaders like the Apostle Paul, Moses, Joshua, and Nehemiah as servants of their people display outwardly that distinguished them from other leaders, both then and now? The Apostle Paul kept his focus to *emulate* Christ and endured all the infirmities and persecutions he suffered to complete his goal to preach the gospel of Jesus Christ. He inspired Timothy and others through his effective *discipleship* leadership to imitate him as he emulated Christ. Moses' outward display of his *trus*t in God's power earned him a good level of trust from the people and empowered him for the mission of delivery of God's children from bondage in Egypt; he had to *reproduce* himself in Joshua to complete the mission. But the greatest of them was Jesus Christ, who humbly sacrificed His life to finish the work of redemption. In His *Servanthood*, commitment, and love for the people, He became the ultimate *model* of a leader as a servant to *emulate*.

Let's consider for a moment secular leaders in these current times! For example, think of Henry Ford, who founded the successful Ford Motor Company; Bill Gates who created the global empire that is Microsoft; Albert Einstein, who in many ways is synonymous with a genius for his contributions to modern physics; Abraham Lincoln, remembered as one of the greatest presidents and leaders of United States; and many others like these we cannot mention. What did all these leaders have in common? What propelled them to turn their initial failures or challenges into eventual successes? None had a direct mentor or inherited any fortune from their parents. Nevertheless, they all eventually succeeded. These people can be distinguished from others based on their self-will to succeed, their self-confidence and belief in themselves, their self-determination, and their perseverance, among other characteristics. The distinguishing characteristics displayed externally in service or relationships toward others are the outward functional attributes that define that leader.

Think about yourself as a student, faculty member, or that new executive. What was it that made your journey to success different and even great? Students and colleagues, when they see or hear about my display of what I have referred to as the 'wilderness walk of faith', have asked me to share the critical attitudinal elements that made me remain inwardly resilient and undaunted and yet outwardly joyful in the difficulties I had faced. This book is the result of those reflections. Let me explain one such teaching moment.

Many years ago, sitting in my research lab on a Saturday morning trying to finish writing my dissertation, a fellow graduate student walked into the room to talk with me. He was contemplating terminating his graduate studies. He was a privileged single male student but felt the load was just too much.

"Sylvanus," he asked, with seriousness in his eyes, "your research advisor suggested that I should ask you, 'what is it that makes you tick?'.'What is it about you that makes you joyful and at peace with yourself and determined to finish, no matter the situations and high expectations we face in this department?"

What he asked me were deeply reflective questions, but I was willing and excited to answer them. Even so, before I do, let's look at the context. At that period in my life, I had four little children as a graduate student; in fact, more children than any of the faculties at that time, except for one faculty member who had eight children. I received little or no support from the department. I was then an international alien, did not qualify for financial aid, and was not given any research assistant position. I was, therefore, self-supported with two off-campus part-time jobs. I joked at being a minority of minorities, the only student in the department with such a label,—but I was self-willed to succeed. My adaptability attribute, coupled with perseverance and resilience, was all that I needed to succeed despite the odds against me. In every exam, homework assignment, or project I had to compete with students with full financial aid, plus they had nothing to distract their attention from their studies. I lived with the attitude that using disadvantages as an excuse was not an option. Aspiring to earn my Ph.D. was a life dream, and I was willing to give my ultimate best to actualize that dream even in the face of challenges. The choice was mine!

So I looked at my classmate and all I could see was a student striding through a valley through which I also walked. He needed me to show him how to walk the walk, to empathize with him. To answer his question, I smiled, not that I wanted to, but because it was just who I was. The joy he attributed to me was an overflow of my appreciation of God's grace that His life in me was externally manifesting His light to bless someone else. It was a great teaching moment; I capitalized on it to tell my classmate that my joy was not about me. He could see physically but about He who was in me, he could not see in the flesh; I needed him to know that I was just showing forth His life in me. At first, my classmate did not understand the spiritual prose or metaphor I was using. He looked surprised but open to hearing more.

I did not ask if he was a Christian. However, right on my desk was my small green pocket Bible. I opened to 2 Corinthians 12:9 (NIV) and handed it to him to read. As he read the passage: "But he said to me, 'My grace is sufficient for you, for my power is made perfect in weakness.' Therefore, I will boast all the more gladly about my weaknesses, so that Christ's power may rest on me," I noticed how absorbed he was in the words

He looked astonished and read it again, this time silently. "This is interesting, but what does this mean?" He asked. I took his question to mean, "How does this relate to my question?

I explained to my friend that the external attitudes he or my advisors saw in me that warranted the question, "What makes you tick" were inspired by my inner value system based on my faith in this same Christ and His teachings. My desire to manifest His life and self-confidence is all because of what He has promised in His word if I believed. I have believed His words and have gained self-determination and faith to make the right choices through Him for my life, and his spirit has given me perseverance and resilience to focus on finishing strong in pursuit of any goal. "With that faith, I have continued, more passionately and excitedly; I can look at my challenges and vulnerabilities and delight joyfully in them, even as an alien minority of minorities! His grace and power have empowered me to do all things I want to do. That is what makes me tick," I explained.

He looked at me as if he got his answer. "Wow, thanks!" he said, looking inspired and ready to face his challenges. As we concluded with a prayer, and he stood up to leave, I pointed empathetically to his face and said, "If I made it despite my challenges, you have absolutely no excuse but to persevere to complete your studies; you can make it too!"

It is fitting to report that this encounter with my classmate transformed his will and determination to continue. Yes, he was encouraged and went on to complete his graduate studies. He emulated self-will and perseverance from the example of the most vulnerable of all students in the department.

The inner value system of a Leader-Servant is founded not only on his faith but his self-will, coupled with self-leadership; it is the greatest mentor who can turn any situation into an inconceivable success. Self-will is the primary driver for determination, resilience, and perseverance. It is what wakes you up in the morning to ask for strength to do whatever it is you are setting out to do. Based on my life walk of faith, I can state with absolute certainty that faith is the unseen assuredness that can empower you to turn your life's probable impossibilities into great and improbable possibilities.

ABOUT LEADER AS SERVANT LEADERSHIP (LSL) MODEL

Looking at the testimony above, do you know the source that energizes the characteristics you display outside and how your inner self is related to what others see outside? What distinguishes you from others is what combines to define your attributes! As a follower, can you identify the characteristics that distinguish your leaders? As an executive, how do you base your evaluation of yourself? Or how do you evaluate that brand-new manager or new youth director you want to hire? To what do you compare the individual's qualities when you look at his CV? What is the basis of your measure? Do you know if you are a substantial leader? These personal questions and much more are the subjects of this two-volume book, 'The Authentic Leader as Servant Part I: The Outward Leadership Attributes, Principles, and Practices', is written in two parts; the second part 'The Leader as Servant Leadership Model. Part II'; deals with the Inner Strength Leadership Attributes, Principles, and Practices.

When we think about today's corporate greed, deepening divide between the haves and have-not, gridlock in political systems, conflicts and wars, high divorce rates, and the rich young ruler in the Bible, it is easy to agree that all these people share a few things in common: self-centeredness, pride, lack of compassion, and greed. There is a great need in today's suffering world for leader-servants who display leadership attributes. These attributes should be oriented toward selfless service to others. Indeed, our world is increasingly drifting away from global serving reality toward the self and apathy. The most credible message or model for a possible solution to this dilemma and the answer to several complex leadership questions can be found in the foundation of the ultimate leader-servant, Jesus Christ. This book defines the Leader as Servant Leadership attribute as the combined acts of two or more distinctive functional leadership characteristics exhibited in service and relationship toward others. There is no better time than now for a book that presents comprehensive and irrevocable facts and principles regarding how to develop effective attributes of the leader-servant.

The Leader as Servant Leadership Model

My first book on this subject, The Leader as Servant Leadership Model, explains that Jesus' servant leadership model is based on the notion of a Leader as a Servant and not on a Servant as Leader. There are four distinct differences between a Servant as Leader (Servant-leader) and the Leader as Servant (leader--servant) models. It is pertinent to highlight them here to connect to this book, Authentic Leader as Servant.

A Leader as Servant is a leader first. The leader–servant as a leader does not in the line of duty go projecting or lording his or her power and authority over others but is the person to lead the process of influencing desired changes in others through his humble example of being a servant or having a serviceable attitude toward others. He or she is a serving leader, not a lording leader. He leads as a servant by putting others' needs above his own needs and rights. Jesus emphasized the word "as" meaning that the leader (the Master) chooses to serve as a servant even though he is the leader. A leader–servant emulates Jesus, who gave up all rights, and emptied and expended Himself on His followers. He empowered them to become more like Him. A leader-servant is known as a leader first but is seen as a great leader by his humble attendant heart and acts of service to others. His greatness comes from his ability to put others above himself.

Leader as Servant is a Biblical Concept. The model or image of a humble serving leader motivated Jesus' disciples to see that if their master could do this for them, they must also be able to do it for others. Jesus clearly demonstrated the process of leader-as-servant leadership. In some cases, He chose to serve by leading when He wanted to create the image or model of the leader-servant in certain acts. In other cases, He chose to lead by serving, when he showed care and empathy toward the people and led the disciples to see empathy as a leadership attribute.

Leader as Servant is an Authentic Leadership Model to follow. The Leader as the Servant leadership model intentionally positions Jesus as an original model of a leader to follow.

He was serving His disciples to demonstrate that the process of becoming a great leader was earned through humble acts of service to others; He made them understand that He was empowering them to succeed Him as leader-servants through service to others. The result was an incomparable legacy of leadership that changed their communities. The fact that Jesus relinquished his rights or shared His power did not diminish His power and influence. In fact, his influence increased at least 11 X 100%, if we ignore the one case of Judas.

The Leader as Servant Transforms Organizational Culture. The proposed LSL model seeks to transform and sustain the community or organization by instilling key leadership values or "leadership presence" among followers or an organization's members. Change is sustained when everyone in the organization takes ownership of the change. Rather than focusing on leading more followers to be great followers who conform to the organizational culture, LSL seeks to lead and empower better leaders to be distinguished leaders and community builders.

There are four distinctions, which clearly differentiate many of the existing servants as Leader-based philosophies in relation to servant leadership from my LSL model. Even in the corporate or institutional worlds, there is nothing better than Jesus on which to base Servant Leadership. There is nothing more authentic and impacting than the servant leadership modeled by the life and teachings of Jesus Christ.

The LSL model uses exploratory questions, scenarios, and graphic visualizations to excite critical thinking in ways no other book on this subject has yet attempted. Several personal testimonies of my wilderness walk of faith with God are used to connect the reader to real-life experiences of the concepts discussed. The riveting effect is that the text engages and encourages the reader to walk through the experiences presented. The aim is to inspire the reader spiritually, mentally, and professionally with this far-reaching exposition on the subject of servant leadership.

ABOUT THE AUTHENTIC LEADER AS SERVANT (ALS)

The *Authentic Leader as Servant* argues that no leadership model is as authentic, other-centered, able to build communities, and productive and service-oriented as the model of our ultimate leader-servant, Jesus Christ. No source can provide a better point of reference than that provided in the Bible. Hence, this book aims to be more than just a text on leadership; it hopes to be a personal discovery for those who aspire to develop effective leadership attributes that grow leaders as servants who ultimately develop thriving other-centered communities. This book presents a comprehensive, biblically-based study regarding how to develop these attributes and how they are applied in a servant leadership process. In this biblical context and for clarity, Servant Leadership means *Leader-as-Servant Leadership*. A *leader-servant* refers to a *leader as a servant*, which is distinct from a servant-leader or servant as leader.

Leader as Servant Leadership attributes are shaped by the Leadership's Inner Value system, which consists of character, motivation, and commitment. The *Authentic Leader as Servant* is presented as a necessary resource to complement my *The Leader as Servant Leadership (LSL) Model*. The LSL model integrates a transformative leadership framework and interactive dimensions of Servant Leadership. Leader as Servant Leadership is a process in which a leader, in his leadership position, purposefully chooses to put others' rights and needs above his positional rights and personal needs. He then serves, enables, and empowers followers for growth that builds a thriving organization. The LSL model looks at the predominant Servant Leadership concepts and shares how they compare with biblical principles on how we should lead and be led.

ALS ENCOURAGEMENT LEADERSHIP
ATTRIBUTES, PRINCIPLES, & PRACTICES

ABOUT THE ALS COURSES

The three books, *LSL Model* and *The Authentic Leader as Servant (*Parts I and II), together demonstrate that with today's global visions to reach people of all races and cultures, now is the time for an authentic servant's heart of service. Those visions and the leadership processes are most effective with the appropriate leadership attributes centered more on people than on the organization, principles regarding how to develop effective attributes of leader-servant.

The ALS I and II combined presented twenty leaders as servant leadership attributes. The series of ALS courses supply training guide to understand, develop, and practice the attributes in a leadership process. Each course is independent and self-contained and does not depend on completing any other course in the series of 20 courses. It is, however strongly recommended, in fact a must read, that chapters 1 and 2 in each series be covered as they lay the foundation of LSL model on which ALS is based.

ALS (Parts I & II) Course Layout

The *Authentic Leader as Servant (ALS)* leadership (parts I and II) book has been broken down into 20 courses in workbook format to achieve three goals 1) Self-discovery of the acts of developing the attribute under review in the course, 2) deeper understanding of the principles, research and biblical teaching behind the attributes, and 3) Learning the strategies for practicing the attributes.

Instruction

The set of questions following each chapter are designed to serve as a guide to discover, explore, and practice the essential ALS leadership attributes, principles, and practices in leadership process. The questions are comprehensive review based on the content of this specific chapter only.

To maximize the learning outcomes, the learner must read through this chapter and sections. Some referenced scriptures in the book are repeated in the summaries for added review if needed, even though they were discussed in the section in which they apply.

> The exercises that follow each chapter will help you in not only understanding your own strength and weaknesses in your acts of the attribute but will guide you in developing practical strategies you can apply in self-leadership process or helping others grow in leadership
>
> All answers to the questions are contained in the associated chapter or sections; consultation of new sources, except for the reference scriptures, is not needed. Thus, it is expected that you answer the questions after you have read the associated section or chapter of the workbook. The scripture or other references cited are only for references as they already discussed in the book

ALS II Course 1: Adaptability Leadership Attribute—*Flexibility overcomes rigidity in new and changing situations.*

Adaptability is framed as an inner strength quality of a leader in responding to changing needs or situations in a service mission. According to the Army training Handbook, adaptability is "an individual's ability to recognize changes in the environment, identify the critical elements of the new situation, and trigger changes accordingly to meet new requirements." God showed Moses adaptability when he empowered him to use the rod in his hand as an instrument for the mission ahead of him. This course will attempt to give meanings to personal reflective questions to discover the distinguishing characteristics of Leadership Adaptability. Numerous techniques, personal examples, empirical case studies, and applications of the adaptability developing strategies are discussed concepts. Practice questions at the end of each chapter are used to guide your development and to frame meanings out of the content to improve your acts of adaptability in a leadership process.

ALS II Course 2: Courage Leadership Attribute—*Courage is the inner strength of the mind to triumph over paralyzing fears of purposeful action that yields good success*

Courage Leadership Attribute is the lynchpin of effective Servant Leadership that supports the display of all the other attributes? Having the inner strength of character and convictions to persevere and hold on to new and often misunderstood ideas in the face of opposition takes courage—inner strength to triumph over the fear of failure or danger. It is even greater courage to venture into positions or overcome situations that nobody like you, has gone to before or where many better qualified than you had gone and failed. In all cases, they all display courage in the face of obstacles and uncertainties. The success is more about courage than the experience. Can such courage be learned or inspired? How do leaders or successful people in their callings get to their heights of achievements? How can courage be an inner strength within or beyond leadership? How does courage attribute triumph over paralyzing fear? This course explores answers to these questions and more by searching for the distinguishing characteristics of courage. Numerous techniques, personal examples, empirical case studies, including practice questions at the end of each chapter are used to guide your development and to frame meanings out of the content to improve your acts of courage leadership process.

ALS II Course 3: Empathy Leadership Attribute—*A measure of a leader's compassion is the empathic engagement in a follower's experience and state of well-being beyond just expressions of feelings and concerns.*

Empathy attribute is the ability to project one's personality and experiences into another person's thoughts, emotions, direct experience, position, and act toward the wellness of that person. How can a leader walk along with someone in that individual's "wilderness" state of suffering or danger? What motivates a leader to *empathize* with a follower? How is empathy an inner strength leadership attribute? Whether it's in your church, your business, your institution, or in your community, this course provides a comprehensive biblical-based discussion on the role of a leader as a servant in empathizing with those he leads. The aim is to inspire the reader spiritually, mentally, and professionally with this far-reaching exposition on empathy in servant leadership. How can a leader make a lasting positive impact in the lives of those he or she leads? Answers to these and other personal reflective questions are explored in this course on Leadership Empathy Attributes. Numerous techniques, personal examples, empirical case studies, including practice questions at the end of each chapter are used to guide your development and to frame meanings out of the content to improve your acts of empathy leadership process.

ALS II Course 4: Encouragement Leadership Attribute—*The direct measures of encouragement are the inspired strength and quality of uplifted spirit to persevere toward a desired outcome.*

There are times when people want to grow in their potential, want to change their present situation, feel emotionally low in lived experiences, or feel as if they should be appreciated for a job well done. In any of these cases, some encouragement goes a long way to lift up the spirit of someone low. A case study is of the leadership qualities of Barnabas, named the "Son of Encouragement" by the disciples (Acts 4:36), because they saw him as an *encourager.* You can only be an encourager from the strength of your inner personality. The act of encouragement is mostly expressed or *given* to inspire growth or apply a spiritual gift to serve others. What did the disciples see in Barnabas? Obviously, he must have affected them with his acts of encouragement. They saw him as an encourager by his *courage* to *inspire* them at a time they desperately needed to move the ministry forward. This course explores the distinguishing characteristics of encouragement attributes in servant leadership. Each characteristic of encouragement attribute will be discussed in detail with emphasis on strategies of how they can be further developed or practiced by a leader-servant in a leadership process. Practice questions at the end of each chapter are used to guide your development and to frame meanings out of the content to improve your acts of encouragement leadership process.

ALS II Course 5: Initiation Leadership Attribute—*Initiation creates the catalyst for a vision, and the vision when acted upon, produces a desired change.*

The initiation of a process for a desired change is the core of the inner strength of a decisive leader in any leadership process. Initiation leadership is the act of taking step to originate or get something started. In general, initiative is an "individual's action that begins a process, often done without direct managerial influence." The primary outcome of the initiation attribute is that it leads to desired change; something new in the lives of the followers or organization, such as a new growth in followers, a new product or policy in an organization, or a new mission or mission agenda. How do leaders take action to begin a process of change? What are the distinguishing initiation characteristics of leaders such as Moses and Nehemiah in working according to God's agenda? How does a leader conceive a strategic vision for initiation action?. or negotiate his way to influence possible actions toward that vision. This course explores answers to these, and other questions based on examples from Nehemiah (Nehemiah 1:4 through 2:6-8) and Moses and God (Exodus 3 and 4:1-14).

ALS II Course 6: Listening Communication Leadership Attribute —*Effective communication occurs at the convergence of listening attention, hearing, and understanding of the information transmitted.*

A leader-servant face three important types of communication at one point or the other. At the core is listening ability as the inner strength and ability to receive and understand the meanings of words and messages internally and accurately in a two-way communication process. How does a leader-servant communication with God, the Holy Spirit, and followers (individually or collectively) to be most effective. The course explores how the three elements—words spoken, unspoken, and in the spirit—offer unique reflections of the communication process and what they share in common. How does listening serve as a critical element of effective communication between people forms the bridge by which a leader can be effective?. A leader's capacity to listen to communicate effectively depends on the leader's inner strength to perceive, hear, and understand the information from written, verbal, and non-verbal exchanges. Each characteristic of listening communications attribute will be discussed in detail with emphasis on strategies of how they can be further developed or practiced by a leader-servant. Practice questions at the end of each chapter are used to guide your development and to frame meanings out of the content to improve your acts of listening leadership process.

ALS II Course 7: Navigation Leadership Attribute—*Leaders who prepare for and chart through a purposeful course of action arrive with their followers at the desired destination.*

The navigation attribute is having a *vision* for the intended destination plus the direction to get there. Having a vision is a quality of the inner strength of a leader and the path that the leader follows in the life journey is often influenced by internal and external factors. The organizational culture and climate collectively combine to make an organization unique through the diversity of employees' characteristics, values, needs, attitudes, and expectations. How does a leader-servant *navigate* and *negotiate* his actions through the organization and people he serves, individually or collectively, to *finish* or *arrive* at his purpose? How do you prepare your followers to *finish* strong or *arrive* at their destinations? This course explores answers to these and other questions and how a leader's inner strength capacity can empower him to navigate the cultural bridges to influence the desired change in others in their personal and professional needs and attitudes.

ALS II Course 8: Responsibility Leadership Attribute—*Leadership responsibility is the measure of the quality of a Leader's accountability for the growth of followers and the organization*

Responsibility leadership refers to possessing the capability and accountability needed in the act of being responsible (trustworthy, dependable, honest, etc.) in a leadership process. At a personal level, it defines the level of your position (pastor, deacon, department head, janitor, etc.) in your church, family, or employment. Responsible leaders in their positions *choose* to emphasize the positive, uplifting, and flourishing side of organizational life. Are there qualities in your position that need to be trained or developed to influence positive outcomes in people and organizations? Organizationally, what are the attributes of the leadership structure, process, and culture that are most conducive for maximizing the growth of followers and organizations in service toward others? How can responsibility qualities be developed to enhance high-quality relationships, emotional competencies, positive communication, beneficial energy development, and positive climates for the effective leader as a servant leadership process? The course explores answers to these and other questions. Distinguishing leadership characteristics of responsibility attributes are identified and discussed in detail. Practice questions at the end of each chapter are used to guide your development and to frame meanings out of the content to improve your acts of responsibility leadership process.

ALS II Course 9: Stewardship Leadership Attribute—*A measure of good stewardship is the entrustments' better and richer growth change at the end than at the beginning*

S*tewardship leadership is the process of u*tilizing and managing the resources entrusted to you by someone. We recognize that God has ownership of everything above, and below the earth. In that context, we are all stewards of what God owns, including our lives but entrusted to us to be managed and maintained in a purposeful manner that will honor God. What are the distinctive servant leadership characteristics of stewardship and how can they be developed? This course explores answers to these questions with reference to servant leadership. Practice questions at the end of each chapter are used to guide your development and to frame meanings out of the content to improve your acts of steward leadership process

ALS II Course 10: Vision Leadership Attribute—*You have a vision when you understand how you get to your mission-purpose and what the future outcome will be relative to your present.*

The vision leadership attribute gives the leader the ability to specify in the present *what* each follower's or group's growth should be in the future, *where* to focus these efforts to meet that growth; *how* he will accomplish all aspects of his mission, *which* future (destination) he aspires to lead the people, and *when* the purpose will be achieved. Leadership without direction leads followers to nowhere. Vision is the most common descriptor of effective leadership and must be clear and inspirational in order to achieve desired purpose. What are the qualities a visionary leader? When was the last time you added brand new challenges to your normal routine to achieve a new you? Answers to these and other questions are explored in this course. The primary characteristics of visionary leadership will be identified and used to frame a principle of leadership vision attribute. Practice questions at the end of each chapter are used to guide your development and to frame meanings out of the content to improve your acts of encouragement leadership process.

Referenced Scriptures

A variety of Bible translations from over 11,200 original Hebrew, Aramaic, and Greek words to about 6,000 English words do exist with variations in meanings and emphases. I am not a biblical scholar and do not pretend to be one; Hence, I have avoided researching the roots of these words and personally prefer New King James Version (NKJV). I have intentionally used other translations for three main reasons; first, to allow for increased impact and alignment of words to the most desired meaning and emphasis in the concepts being addressed. Second, I wanted new and personal discovery of meanings from translations with which I have not been familiar. And third, I wanted to allow readers who may desire translations other than the NKJV the benefit of their preferred translations. Hence, in addition to the NKJV, other translations used in the book include New International Version (NIV), New Living Translation (NLT), King James Version (KJV), English Standard Version (ESV), and Good News Translation (GNT). Unless otherwise specified, NKJV should be assumed.

Sylvanus Nwakanma Wosu

CHAPTER 1
UNDERSTANDING LEADERSHIP ATTRIBUTES

Leadership attribute is the combined acts of two or more distinctive functional leadership characteristics exhibited in service and relationship toward others.

The starting point of our discussion is the understanding of the key functional definitions and concepts that describe the theme of this book. In general, 1 will define leadership as an integrative process in which a person applies appropriate attributes to guide and influence the sought-after attitudinal changes in others toward accomplishing a particular goal. Specifically, the Leader as Servant Leadership is a process in which a leader intentionally chooses to put the follower's rights and needs above his positional rights and personal needs, and serves, enables, and empowers them for desired spiritual and professional growth that builds thriving communities.

FUNCTIONAL DEFINITIONS

In the context of these definitions, I will begin the descriptions of the leadership attributes of an authentic leader-servant by offering a functional definition of Leadership Attributes, and showing how that definition differs from those of Leadership Character, Characteristics, and Traits.

Leadership Character is the sum total of personal qualities in leadership, such as honesty, values, vision, trust, and so on that make up the moral capital of the leader; Leadership character should describe who the leader is inside or the leader's basic personality traits.

The Leadership Characteristics describe the distinctive characteristics or features of a leader, such as attitudes, competencies, skills, and specific experiences that go beyond his character (personality). Leadership characteristics determine how (through skills and competencies) the leader leads or take actions in the process of leadership in any particular situation;

The Leadership traits are the distinguishing leadership characteristics of a leader (these are things that define his leadership characteristics), which differentiate from personality traits... Leadership traits are the set of characteristics that define a particular leader's leadership. This means that a leadership characteristic is a trait when it is a unique characteristic of the leader.

Leadership Attributes, unlike leadership character, characteristics, and traits, is *a leadership attribute and the combined act of two or more distinctive functional leadership characteristics exhibited in service and relationship toward others* or traits externally displayed in action toward others. All leadership attributes grow out of the leadership inner value system but can be externally displayed predominantly as an outbound or outward attribute or both:

1. **Outbound Attributes:** These are distinctive outward-bound attributes emanating from the inner strength of the leader to support external conduct in service and relationships toward others. They form the internal core functional qualities that motivate or enhance the outward manifestation of the inside character toward others. The outbound attribute such as listening and vision, for example, are the direct results of the inner values of the leader such as patience, hearing, love, humility, or all the fruits of the spirit.

2. **Outward Attributes:** These are distinctive functional outward outer visible attributes emanating from the richness of the outbound and inner values of the leader. For example, external attributes such as Servanthood, emulation/modeling, empathy, etc. are outflows from the leader who will directly impact the follower. Outward attributes can be enriched by the outbound (inner) attributes. As shown in Figure 1, the outward attributes in general form the outer core of

functional attributes in the leader as servant leadership, but they can share some overlapping functions with the outbound attributes.

Figure 1.1. Servant leadership functional attributes

In summary, a leadership attribute is more than an ability or a characteristic; it is making those characteristics or abilities functional as part of how the leader acts (his habits) in service to others and applying those characteristics (beyond just having them) in personal and service relations to others. The character or known characteristic defines some aspects of your abilities or who you are inside— e.g. honest, humble, brave, etc. Your attribute, on the other hand, defines your habits; a display of how you use your characteristics, or the actions you exhibit toward others because of who you are inside. For example, empathy as a leadership characteristic becomes a leadership attribute if the followers can distinguish the leader's acts or habits of empathy, such as walking through with his followers in their state of suffering to bring wholeness; otherwise, it is just a characteristic or ability. Leadership attributes toward others are what impact the followers' and the organizational growth more than ability and competence.

In addressing one of the self-righteous hypocritical attributes of servitude leadership, Jesus called leader-servants to be "inside-out" leaders that reflect credibility; indeed, leaders should not appear outwardly righteous when they are full of hypocrisy and lawlessness in their hearts. He was describing "inside–out" as an authentic leadership attribute measured by the display of credibility a leadership attribute!

The measuring stick of a leader-servant is Jesus Christ. We measure ourselves unto the measure of the status of the fullness of Christ (Ephesians 4:13).

The leadership attributes of an authentic leader as a servant are encapsulated in **SERVANT/SERVING LEADERSHIP** are listed in Table 1.1, and defined in Table 1.2: *Servanthood, Emulation, Responsibility, Vision, Navigation, Adaptability, Trust, Listening, Empathy, Affection, Discipleship, Encouragement, Reproduction, Stewardship, Healing-Care, Initiation, Integrity,* and *Persuasion*. Other support attributes include *Influence, Courage, and Generosity*.

The attributes have been separated into Outward and Outbound (Inner Strength) leadership Attributes. As shown in Table 1.1, each of these attributes has three or more leadership characteristics. As such, more than 65 leadership characteristics are covered in these 20 attributes. For example, a leader's Servanthood leadership attribute is characterized by his willing servant's heart of selfless role humility, sacrifice, and submissiveness. The more these are present in a leader, the more effective the servant leadership.

Table 1.1: The functional leader-servant leadership Outbound (Inner Strength) and Outward attributes

	LEADER-SERVANT LEADERSHIP ATTRIBUTES			INNER STRENGTH ATTRIBUTES	OUTWARD ATTRIBUTES
S	Servanthood	**L**	Listening	Adaptability	Affection
E	Emulation	**E**	Empathy	Courage	Discipleship
R	Responsibility	**A**	Affection	Empathy	Emulation
V	Vision	**D**	Discipleship	Encouragement	Generosity
A	Adaptability	**E**	Encouragement	Initiation	Healing-Care
N	Navigation	**R**	Reproduction	Listening	Influence
T	Trust	**S**	Stewardship	Navigation	Persuasion
I	Influence	**H**	Healing-Care	Responsibility	Reproduction
G	Generosity	**I**	Initiation	Stewardship	Servanthood
C	Courage	**P**	Persuasion	Vision	Trust/Integrity

The list does not assume that a leader has to be excellent in all attributes or even have all of them to be an effective Leader–Servant. However, the more of these attributes the leader displays in his acts of service toward others, the more productive he or she will be, and the further his impact on the followers and organization. The table also shows that two or more attributes can share common characteristics, which can be applied or observed in different contexts. For example, a leader's ability to inspire followers can be seen in his acts of discipleship, empowerment, an.d encouragement attributes in the context in which these attributes apply. Each attribute is exhibited either as a part of the outbound inner strength attribute of a leader or a part of the outward attribute. Table 1.1 is not an exhaustive list of attributes; in fact, there are hundreds of such attributes. This is just the starting point.

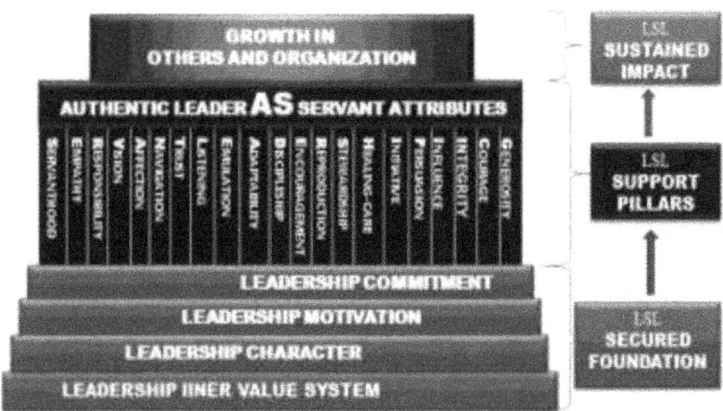

Figure 1.2: Servant leadership outward attributes (dark blue) and relationship to four foundational layers of the LSL Model

Figure 1.2 shows that the leader's attributes are shaped and secured by his four foundational layers (leadership inner value system, leadership character, motivation, and commitment). The attributes of the leader–servants are also conceptualized as the support pillars that will establish and support the personal authenticity of the leader, what the leader, does and the effectiveness of the leadership process. Thus, the attributes represent functional pillars of authentic leadership that can be learned or enriched as described in detail in the subsequent chapters. The combined effect of a secured foundation and stable support pillars will make a sustained impact on the growth of followers and the organization.

COMPARISONS WITH OTHER WORKS

The original works by Greenleaf (1970) in servant leadership [1] have been reviewed by Larry Spears (1996), who identified listening, empathy, healing, awareness, persuasion, conceptualization, foresight, stewardship, commitment to the growth of others, and building community as the ten distinguishing characteristics of servant leadership. [2] Russell (2001) has studied these attributes and have shown them to be essential in servant leadership and concluded that these qualities generally "grow out of the inner values and beliefs of individual leaders." [3] Russell and Stone (2002) extended the Greenleaf 10 attributes to 20 attributes observed in servant-leaders. These 20 attributes were categorized by these authors as either functional attributes (intrinsic characteristics of servant-leaders) or accompanying attributes (complement attributes that enhance the functional attributes).[4] The operational attributes were identified as vision, honesty, integrity, trust, modeling, service, pioneering, appreciation, and empowerment with the accompanying attributes of communication, credibility, competence, stewardship, visibility, influence, persuasion, listening, encouragement, teaching, and delegation. Only three of the attributes identified by Greenleaf were identified, and all three were accompanying attributes rather than functional. Responsibility, adaptability, affection, discipleship, navigation, and reproduction attributes which are considered critical in biblical-based servant leadership in my LSL model are not covered by Russell and Greenleaf. As shown in the description of the attributes in Table 1.2, most of the attributes reported by Russell and Stone (2002)[5] or Greenleaf [1] can be seen either in the twenty attributes or their associated characteristics. Integrity and honesty for example are leadership characteristics of trust and other attributes rather than an independent attributes. I take the position that servant leadership attributes are functional attributes in acts of duty to others and emanate from the inner value system of the leader.

CHAPTER 1
UNDERSTANDING LEADERSHIP ATTRIBUTES

Table 1.2: Description of the functional leader-servant outward leadership attributes and associated principles and characteristics

Leader–Servant Leadership Attributes	Principles of Leadership Attributes	Leadership Characteristics
Affection: *This is the combined love-based works toward providing the essential help or services for the spiritual growth or survival of another person.* . (Chapter 2)	*Affection flows from a person to produce positive emotions for the well-being of another person*	Kindness Compassion Practical Love Affective signs Appreciation
Discipleship: *This is the combined acts of personally developing, intentionally equipping, and attentively empowering growth in others to reproduce a heart of service.* (Chapter 3)	*Discipleship transforms and empowers followers for service leadership that grows communities.*	Inspiring Shepherding Equipping Developing Empowering
Emulation: *This is the combined acts of initiating an authentic servant attitude as a model of service worthy of following* (Chapter 4)	*A great leader-servant outwardly and positively inspires a pattern of good works for others to follow.*	Inspiration Motivation Initiation Model Following
Generosity: *This is the combined acts of freely sharing with and giving to others as an act of kindness, without expectation of reward or return to him.* (Chapter 5)	*Generosity is an outward measure of the level of sacrifice, what is shared, or the impact a giving makes, not just the size of the giving.*	Sharing Giving Kindness Affection Love
Healing-Care: *This is the combined acts of providing comfort and empathy to make others whole emotionally and spiritually along with tending to the follower's physical and mental well-being.* (Chapter 6)	*Comforting others in any trouble with the comfort with which we are comforted by God, brings healing - wholeness.*	Self-Healing Empathy Reconciliation Comfort Relational
Influence: *This is the combined acts of positively affecting desired change in conduct,*	*The true measure of leadership success in affecting*	Model Positive attitude Authority

performance, and relational connections toward others-centered course of action or service. (Chapter 7)	desired change in conduct, performance, and relational connections in others is influence	Connection Wisdom Intelligence,
Persuasion: This is the combined acts of communicating perspective to connect, challenge, and convince with a compelling purpose to convert others to a new position. (Chapter 8)	The means of transforming others to a new perspective is through empathetic persuasion	Connecting Challenging Communicating Convincing Converting Encouraging
Reproduction: This is the combined acts of developing your leadership qualities in others and releasing them as successors to continue a greater mission. (Chapter 9)	Great leaders produce successors for legacy and greater courses as an expected product of an effective leadership reproduction.	Selecting Mentoring Equipping Empowering Releasing
Servanthood: This is the combined acts of humility, willingness, and intentionality in service to others through selfless sacrifice and submission as a servant. (Chapter 10)	A leader-servant is most qualified to lead when most ready to serve as a servant for the growth of others. The role of a leader is to serve as a servant	Servant's heart Humility Sacrifice Service Willingness Submissiveness
Trust: This is the combined acts of positive display of character, competence, credibility, and shared relational connections that produce assured trust-confidence of the trustee in the trusted. (Chapter 11)	True leadership trust produces assured trustee's confidence and readiness to follow based on the credibility, competence, and shared relational connections of the trusted.	Character Competence Integrity Credibility Confidence

PRINCIPLE OF LEADERSHIP ATTRIBUTE

In the context of servant leadership, a leadership attribute is a level above the leadership characteristic or trait of a leader. The principle of leadership attribute states that every leadership attribute has a set of distinguishing characteristics that make up the inward or outward display of the attribute. The principle reflects the essential designed purpose or outcome of the attribute or the inevitable consequence of the effective practice of the attribute. Thus, the principle of leadership attribute is a concise statement about the fundamental truth, value, or belief about the attribute in a leadership situation; it is a statement that establishes an idea about the outcome of the attribute for guiding the practical application of the attribute and its characteristics. I will postulate and frame each principle as an additive function of the characteristics of the attribute. A statement of each principle is quoted at the beginning or below the title of each chapter. It is yet to be experimentally proven if the attribute is a linear or some other non-linear function of these characteristics as variables. It is expected, however, that each character will contribute to the effectiveness of the attribute in varying degrees.

AUTHENTIC LEADERSHIP ATTRIBUTES

At a personal level, attributes are the value-based inside-out moral leadership assets that can be related to the authenticity of a leader-servant. The complexity of defining authenticity has been noted in the literature. The subject of authentic leadership is well covered in the works of Terry (1993),[5] George (2003),[6] and Shair and Eilam (2005).[7] All appear to agree that authenticity requires self-awareness and objective self-identity in personal and social interactions with others. In his book, *Advocacy Leadership*, Professor Gary L. Anderson offers individual, organizational, and societal perspectives on authenticity: "Authenticity, at a peculiar level, is living a life, whether in the private or professional term. This is congruent with one's espoused values; at the structural level, authenticity has to do with viewing human beings as ends in themselves, rather than means to other ends; at the public level, it is a state of affairs that is congruous with the shared political and cultural values of society."[8]

The basic tenets of these perspectives are very fitting to authenticity as a qualifying element of leader-servant leadership attributes. The attribute reflects how the followers see the leader based on the leader's distinctive features displayed through his or her actions personally, organizationally, and societally. The leader is seen as a leader-servant or serving leader because the followers see him lead as a servant from an inside-out value of others. This is what makes the leader authentic.

Authenticity means that what a leader displays outside, in personal or leadership life of service to others, and society is based on the values the leader espouses inside.

Authenticity in servant leadership can be one or two types or both: *Outbound Authenticity and Outward Authenticity*. The Outbound (outward-bound) Authenticity is the genuineness of personal honesty from your inner strength and abilities; what you say and how you act emanate from who you are or how you feel inside. It reflects the essential truth and honesty about your outward-bound inner strength.

Outward authenticity, on the other hand, describes the truthfulness of your credibility and honesty displayed outward in relation to others; your *outer* visible behavior or how you act outwardly towards others reflects exactly your true intentions.

While *outward* authenticity is the visible *outer* indicator of the truth of who you are inside, *outbound* authenticity is outward-bound attribute from the inside of who you are. Credibility in this context is the influence a leader has to attract believability, trustworthiness, and authenticity; it is the believability, trustworthiness, and authenticity of who you are inside and outside.

A key element of personal authenticity is that it is seen or measured in the context of societal, cultural, and organizational interactions. In that context, achieving individual authenticity becomes a challenge since it is influenced by social factors and dispositions of individuals who usually depend on liberal and organizational realities. However, for leader-servant leadership, the leader can face those changing times by remaining focused on his key Biblical-based principles or *Leadership Inner Value System*. Thus, I am interested in authenticity as an essential element of effective Leader-servant leadership attributes or Leader-servant leadership attributes as drivers of leadership authenticity. With that in mind, the first critical element of authenticity in practicing or developing efficient leader-servant leadership attributes is inside-out self-examination relative to the people served rather than the organization. You may ask yourself: What will be my response when the people I lead act or react in a certain way, will it be negative or positive? What are my strengths and vulnerabilities at those times?

Professor Yacobi in his post, "Elements of Human Authenticity," noted that since "the self -arise attribute emerges from interactions between self, others, and the environment in a complex society and world, there may co-exist multiple complicated identities depending on place and context." [9] He went on to identify the following <u>essential elements of personal authenticity</u>: self-awareness, unbiased self-examination, accurate self-knowledge, reflective judgment, personal responsibility, and integrity, genuineness, and humility, empathy for others, understanding of others, optimal utilization of feedback from others. All of these are covered under the leadership attributes or characteristics shown in Table 1.2.

Bill George, in his book, *Authentic Leadership*, takes the position that to be an authentic leader; a person must have the following essential characteristics: [10]

- Behavior based on value: He must understand his own values and exhibit behavior to others based on those values;
- He must not compromise his values in difficult situations but could use the situation to strengthen personal values in those situations.
- Passion from a clear purpose: Be self-aware of who he is, where he is going, and the right thing to do.
- Compassion from the heart: He must lead from a compassionate heart that allows them to be sensitive to the plight and needs of others,
- Connectedness from a relationship; he must be relationally connected with people he leads,
- Consistency from the self-disciple: He must demonstrate self-discipline to remain calm, collected, and consistent in a stressful situation.

Modeled after the elements above, Table 1.3 lists six essential characteristics of authenticity for servant leadership. These fundamental characteristics cover the five identified above and can also be aligned with the leadership characteristics in Table 1.2. Each attribute in Table 1.2 is expected to pass the personal authenticity test in Tables 1.3, 1.4. In a survey of 132 Christian leaders, seventy-four percent (74%) of them agreed that they always or frequently exhibit servant leadership attributes. [11] Thus, a pass of the outward authenticity test means that a pure leader must demonstrate 70% or more of these essential elements of this legitimacy. (That is, 70% YES in the assessment questions in Tables 1.3, 1.4).

It needs to be noted, however, that a secular leader could be authentic and still lack some of the essential servant leadership attributes or characteristics such as selflessness, servanthood, and love-motivated servant attitudes of a leader-servant. Effective leader-servants are authentic leaders and personal authenticity is an essential element of leader-servant leadership. The key test for leader-servant authenticity is the quality of his inside-out value and personal character. What is most important is a change from the inside-out.

Table 1.3: The test of essential elements of personal inner strength authenticity in servant leadership			
	Elements of Inner Strength Authenticity	Inner Strength (Outbound) Authenticity Assessment Questions	YES / NO
1	Personal inside-out value-based behavior	Are your personal inside-out values aligned with acts of service and behavior outside?	1
		Are you honest to yourself in relation to your inner strengths and abilities?	2
2	Inside-out Self-Awareness	Do you have unbiased self-examination, and accurate self-knowledge of who you are inside-out?	3
		Do you know your inner strength and weaknesses in relation to the good you want to show as an outward attribute?	4
3	Inside-out Empathy-Compassion	Do you know and feel from your inside what you want for your followers?	5
		Are you motivated to empathize, based on your inside feelings?	6
4	Inside-out Connection with followers	Do you feel deep, personal, and spiritual connection with your followers?	7
		Does what you say and how you act reflect how you feel when you relate to others?	8
5	Inside-out Emotional Self-regulation	Do you have difficulty controlling your emotion in order to remain calm in a stressful situation?	9
		Are you always able to comfort yourself?	10
6	Inside-out Authenticity Feedback	Do your followers see your inside-out value from your outside behavior?	11
		Will your followers feel that what you say you are is congruent with how you act?	12
#YESs____ ; # NOs____ : Outbound Authenticity: YES/ 12-----%			

Table 1.4: The test of essential elements of personal outward authenticity in servant leadership			
	Elements of Personal Outward Authenticity	Personal Outward Authenticity Assessment Questions	YES or NO
1	Personal value-based outward behavior	Are your personal values and beliefs aligned with your acts of service and behavior toward others?	1
		Do you live out your life according to your beliefs?	2
2	Personal Self-Awareness	Do you have clarity of your personal vision and purpose?	3
		Does what you know about yourself accurately describe what others say?	4
3	Personal Outward Empathy-Compassion	Do you apply how you feel to what your followers need?	5
		Do you lead from a compassionate heart and are you sensitive to the plight and needs of others?	6
4	Personal Connection with followers	Do you feel deep, personal connection with your followers?	7
		Does your outward action toward others reflect exactly your true intentions?	8
5	Outward Emotional Self-regulation	Do you have difficulty controlling your emotions to remain calm in a stressful situation?	9
		Does your evaluation of your value of others agree with how valued they feel?	10
6	Personal Authenticity Feedback	Do your followers see your outward acts as true and honest?	11
		Can your followers see other-centeredness in 70% or more of your attributes?	12
#YESs____; # NOs____: Outbound Authenticity: YES/ 12-----%			

SUMMARY 1
UNDERSTANDING LEADERSHIP PROCESS

Before starting this exercise, please read and follow the instruction in the preface of this workbook. Answers to these questions are contained in this chapter. Completion of these exercises after reading the chapter should take 60-90 minutes.

Discovering the Leadership Attributes

1. What is your alternative definition of leadership? In learning to lead, how would you differentiate the following elements:
    a. Leadership.
    b. Leader as servant leadership.
    c. Leadership characteristics.
    d. Leadership attributes.
2. What are the key differences between the Leader as Servant and the Servant as Leader Leadership philosophies?
3. What was the original source of the Servant as Leader (SL)? What was the original source of Leader as Servant (LS)?
4. What is the key framework of a Leader as a Servant Leadership?
5. Authenticity in servant leadership can be one or two types or both *Outbound Authenticity and Outward Authenticity*: Describe a time when you displayed:
    a. The Outbound (outward-bound)—*outbound* authenticity is outward-bound attribute from the inside of who you are.
    b. *The Outward Authenticity*—*outward* authenticity is the visible *outer* indicator of the truth of who you are inside,
6. Describe the key elements of personal authenticity seen or measured in the context of societal, cultural, and organizational interactions.
7. How are the essential characteristics of authentic leader in leadership process in challenging times?
8. How much of a leader-servant are you? Take the personal leader-servant audit in Table 1.5 to self-assess your effectiveness.
9. Based on the questions in Table 1.5, can you identify each of the twenty attributes? What ones did you score 3 ("sometimes") or less than 3? Review and learn and commit to work to improve.

CHAPTER 1
UNDERSTANDING LEADERSHIP ATTRIBUTES

Table 1.5. Leader As Servant-Leadership Audit

A servant-leader in his leadership position purposefully choses to serve and inspire acts of service in others by his example. Select and circle best answer to questions
1=Never: 2=Almost never ; 3=Sometimes; 4=Frequently; 5 =Always

	Servant Leadership assessment questions	Circle no				
1	I am willing and other-centered, and readily chose to serve others as a servant for their personal growth	1	2	3	4	5
2	I model others-centered attitude in my service and relationships and inspire same for others to follow	1	2	3	4	5
3	I have a sense of obligation, willingness, and accountability for the service towards others	1	2	3	4	5
4	I have the foresightedness to specify in the present view what others' growth should be in a given future	1	2	3	4	5
5	I work toward providing the essential help or services for the spiritual growth or survival of the others;	1	2	3	4	5
6	I provide the needed purposeful course of action for how to chart the course to for my followers.	1	2	3	4	5
7	I display external credibility and a strong sense of character based on values, beliefs, and competence;	1	2	3	4	5
8	In communication, I attentively perceive and hear what is communicated, reflectively listen to understand and to be understood	1	2	3	4	5
9	I walk through with others in their state (suffering, emotions, etc.) in a way that provides the needed care and well-being	1	2	3	4	5
10	I have a measure of self-secured flexibility to adapt appropriate attitude to serve all people in different situations	1	2	3	4	5
11	I personally develop, intentionally equip, and attentively nurture spiritually growth in others	1	2	3	4	5
12	My act of bravery instills in others the courage and confidence to follow or persevere in a course of action	1	2	3	4	5
13	I develop my leadership qualities in others as successors to continue in a purposeful mission	1	2	3	4	5
14	I manage , maintain,, and account for all resources entrusted to me and being responsible for the difference my acts make	1	2	3	4	5
15	As a care-giver, I act to comfort and make others whole emotionally	1	2	3	4	5
16	When I see a need, I originate a vision and action, and stay committed to meet that need and desired change	1	2	3	4	5

17	I display a holistic view of an issue to inform, transform or convert others to my view through empathetic persuasion	1	2	3	4	5
18	I freely share what I have sacrificially as an act of kindness to others, without expectation of reward in return	1	2	3	4	5
19	My act of influence is to affect the actions, behavior, opinions, etc., of others based on trust, credibility and relationship	1	2	3	4	5
20	In the face challenges and danger, I act with bravery to overcome fear and take a stand with strength and conviction	1	2	3	4	5
Score Range	Add up the numbers in each column (Total Score____ Check and Understand the key areas to work on					
81-100	Strong Leader-Servant; keep it up, go and train others.					
66-80	Above average Leader-Servant; work 25% of key areas					
50-65	Average but developing; need to work on 50% of key areas					
34-49	Below average leader; work on 75% of key areas					
<34	Not a Leader-Servant; need training in all areas					

CHAPTER 2
ENCOURAGEMENT
LEADERSHIP ATTRIBUTE

The direct measures of encouragement are the inspired strength and quality of uplifted spirit to persevere toward a desired outcome

In the imperfect world in which followers and leaders operate, the stress associated with life issues causes people to undergo periods of lows and highs. Very often in such situations, people become emotionally low, doubtful about their abilities, and in themselves become greatly insecure, especially in those things that are beyond our control; we feel weak inside and think negatively about our future, this will lead to the sentiments of failure inside. The best and most direct way to gain strength is through words of encouragement from someone stronger emotionally, from within you, or from the Word of God. There are also times when people want to grow in their potential, want to change their present situation, or feel as if they should be appreciated for a job well done. When you ask some high school students to consider engineering or technical fields of education, some might say that their teacher told them they would never be engineers because they could not do a particular math problem. How could a failure in one math question or course predict failure in engineering? Many times, these teachers' intentions were not to discourage the students, but in most cases, their attitudes of motivation lacked encouragement. In any of these cases, some encouragement goes a long way to lift up the spirits of someone low inside for whatever reason to persevere if they are suffering or are striving for a higher calling.

This chapter explores the distinguishing characteristics of encouragement attributes in servant leadership. Functional definitions of leadership encouragement attributes and principles will be presented based on those characteristics. Each characteristic of encouragement attribute will be discussed in detail with emphasis on strategies of how they can be further developed or practiced by a leader-servant as part of the servant leadership process.

SERVANT LEADERSHIP ENCOURAGEMENT ATTRIBUTE

A case study of the characteristics of Barnabas or leaders like him could provide teaching tools for developing leaders' encouraging attributes. We read that Barnabas was named "Son of Encouragement" or "Son of Consolation" by the disciples (Acts 4:36). Barnabas was a Levite whose family came from the Island of Cyprus, where some of the Jews of the Diaspora had settled. His Hebrew name was Joseph ("may God increase") or Joses ("He that pardons"). Only later was he called Barnabas by the apostles. All three names reflect the attributes of God, but the most important characteristic was encouragement. He was an *encourager*. What did they see in him? Obviously, he must have impacted them with his acts of encouragement, and his example is a good reference point for emulation. He clearly inspired all of them. They saw him as an encourager by his *courage* to *inspire* them at a time they desperately needed to move the ministry forward. Courage, as we have seen before, is an inner strength quality of a person's mind. Thus, a leader's act of encouragement to inspire a person in a lower emotional state comes from the leader's inner strength and self-security. You can only be an encourager from the strength of your inner personality. The act of encouragement is mostly expressed, such as in words, endorsement, and praise. In such cases it is purely an inside-out strength of a leader, expressed outwardly to strengthen or inspire others. In others, it serves as a purely outward attribute, but most of the time it is expressed from the inner strength of a leader.

Encouragement can also be *given* such as through fostering an environment to inspire growth or applying a spiritual gift to serve others. As Paul reminded us: "We have different gifts, according to the grace given to each of us; if it is serving, then serve; if it is teaching, then teach; if it is to encourage, then give encouragement..." (Romans 12:6-9). The same was referred to by Peter when he said, "Each one should use whatever gift he has received to serve others, faithfully administering God's grace in its various forms...If anyone *serves,* he should do it with the strength God provides, so that in all things God may be praised through Jesus Christ" (1 Peter 4:10-11, NIV).

Research has shown that people can be encouraged to perform by fostering positive relationships in organizations by modeling and providing acts of compassion, collective forgiveness, and expressions of gratitude, as well as by fostering the formation of friendships at work. Studies by Heaphy & Dutton (2004) showed such acts of encouragement produce physiological effects, which motivate people toward higher performance as well as foster virtuous cycles of enriched relationships.[12] What motivates someone to encourage another? How is encouragement an inner strength attribute?

Most encouraging leaders are internally *enthusiastic* and *passionate* about their mission, and they affect their followers with the same enthusiasm. An enthusiastic leader naturally has a positive perspective and will always see the cup as half full rather than half empty. Encouraging leaders also readily look for ways to *appreciate* their followers for their efforts, especially those efforts they see to have the potential for the follower's greatness. Such leaders usually follow up with the follower with *mentoring* to encourage further growth.

The characteristics of Barnabas as an encourager were identified through his inspiring acts of service in *kindness, generosity, courage, compassion,* reconciliation, and *commitment.* A leader's acts of service go to the heart of the followers. The impact the follower's experience often emerges from their feelings toward their leader.

PRINCIPLE OF LEADERSHIP ENCOURAGEMENT ATTRIBUTE

Encouragement was identified as a dimension of *empowerment* in the Leader as Servant Leadership model (LSL).[10] Encouraged followers are more likely to feel empowered for higher productivity and have a higher sense of accomplishment and meaningfulness in an organization. Based on these characteristics, my working definition in the context of the LSL model is as follows:

Servant leadership encouragement attribute is the combined acts of enthusiastically inspiring and affirming others with the courage to follow a new course of action for growth or uplifting the spirits of others with compassion to persevere in life's challenges.

The life challenges in the definition include states of trials, suffering, and impending danger; emotional lows and highs due to such things as losses, health, marital issues, and others. Life challenges could also mean career issues, promotion issues, difficulties to reposition oneself to a new career, extended family issues, and others. Uplifting someone's spirit is a product of the act of exaltation or praise.

An act of compassion or any of these four characteristics (*enthusiasm, affirmation, exaltation, and compassion*) in service to others can easily differentiate a person as a caring and encouraging leader if the leader's impact resulted in any of the following elements: (1) inspired courage and confidence for a new course of action, (2) brought some hope or promise, and (3) uplifted a spirit to persevere. This principle can be expressed as follows:

Servant leadership encouragement principle: The direct measures of encouragement are the inspired strength and quality of uplifted spirit to persevere toward a desired outcome.

As shown in Figure 5, the Leadership encouragement attribute is externally displayed through overlapping gradation acts of *enthusiasm, affirmation, exaltation, and compassion* in service to others, and can be expressed as:

ENTHUSIASM + AFFIRMATION + EXALTATION + COMPASSION = ENCOURAGEMENT

Chapter 2
Encouragement Leadership Attribute

Developing the Acts of Encouragement-Enthusiasm

Encouragement-enthusiasm is the inner clue that holds the other outer three dimensions together; an attitude of enthusiasm is designed to encourage others. Acts of encouragement through affirmation, exaltation, and compassion can only be effective to the extent that the leader's passion is expressed in the process. Enthusiasm is the positive attitude of a leader which allows him to inspire passion in other people in whatever they are doing. Such an attitude contributes to a stimulating work environment as people will gravitate toward such a leader. Encouraging leaders are more about the people than the project and bringing excitement to the atmosphere. That can also bring the desired excitement to projects and encourage high productivity.

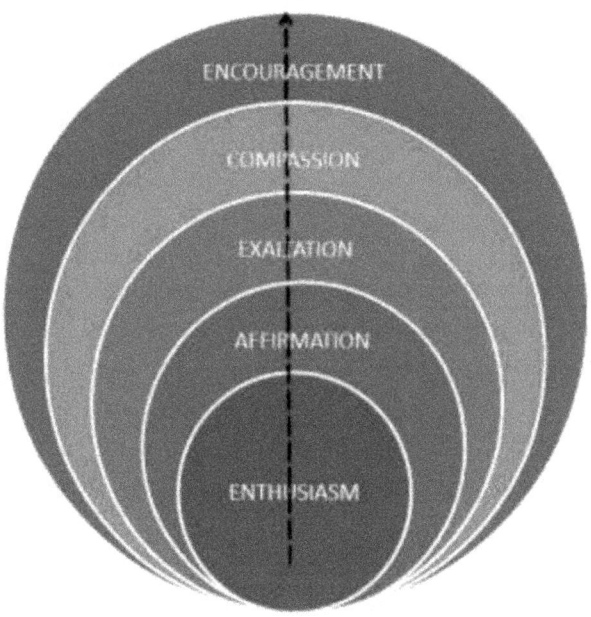

Figure 5: The overlapping gradation models of servant leadership encouragement attribute

An article titled "Mastering Soft Skills for Workplace Success" produced by the U.S. Department of Labor, noted that "When employers look at prospective candidates, beyond skills, experience, and training, they look for those who demonstrate enthusiasm... employers would rather provide job skills training to an enthusiastic but inexperienced worker than hire someone with perfect qualifications but a less-than-positive attitude."[13] The following lessons can be learned from this article:

- Developing a positive attitude starts with learning to believe in one's self. To believe in ourselves, we must first understand our strengths.
- Developing enthusiasm means that we must find ways to empower ourselves to turn negative thinking into positive thinking.
- Enthusiasm for attaining goals is an essential characteristic of success; we must understand that failure is not something to fear and is often a necessary step on the path to success.
- One difference between people with a positive and enthusiastic attitude and people with a negative attitude is that the former look at failure as an opportunity to try again.

Encouragement through exhibiting enthusiastic attitudes of positive belief in oneself, empowering oneself and others, and instilling in followers a positive perspective in handling failure, is very impactful pathways to encourage followers who look up to you as the leader; this will lift up their spirits to persevere in the face of trials, suffering, or in striving for a higher personal purpose

SUMMARY 2
ENCOURAGEMENT LEADERSHIP ATTRIBUTE

Before starting this exercise, please read and follow the instruction in the preface of this workbook. Answers to these questions are contained in this chapter. Completion of these exercises after reading the chapter should take 60-90 minutes.

Discovering Encouragement Leadership Attribute

1. What are distinguishing characteristics of encouragement attributes in servant leadership. In that context provide a functional definitions of encouragement leadership attribute

CHAPTER 2
ENCOURAGEMENT LEADERSHIP ATTRIBUTE

2. Why was Barnabas named "Son of Encouragement" or "Son of Consolation" by the disciples (Acts 4:36). What were the characteristics of Barnabas
3. How were the acts of encouragement expressed? See Paul's teaching in (Romans 12:6-9) or Peter in (1 Peter 4:10-11, NIV).
4. What does research show on how you can encourage person
5. What motivates someone to encourage another? How is encouragement an inner strength attribute?

Understanding the Principle of Encouragement Leadership Attribute

1. State the definition of encouragement leadership attribute in the context of the characteristics of encouragement
2. State the principle of encouragement leadership attribute. What are some life challenges that can benefit from this principle?
3. What four impacts differentiate a leader as an encourager?
4. State the additive law of encouragement leadership attribute.

Practicing Encouragement Leadership Attribute

1. What meaning or lesson can you frame from the experience of reading this chapter?
2. What would you consider the key characteristics of the encouragement leadership attribute?
3. How many acts of encouragement as an attribute do you display?
4. How much of an encourager are you? Find out; take the leadership encouragement Attribute audit in Table AII. 4
5. Based on the questions in Table AII. 4 can you identify each of the characteristic? What ones did you score 3 ("sometimes") or less than 3?
6. Write a personal commitment how to improve.

Encouragement – Enthusiasm provides the inner clue that holds the other outer three dimensions together.
1. Explain how encouragement through affirmation, exaltation, and compassion can be effective.
2. What key positive attitudes can you use as a leader to inspire passion in people in whatever they are working on?

ALS ENCOURAGEMENT LEADERSHIP
ATTRIBUTES, PRINCIPLES, & PRACTICES

Table AII. 4. Leadership Encouragement Attribute Audit

Servant leadership encouragement attribute is the combined acts of enthusiastically inspiring and affirming others with the courage to follow a new course of action for growth or uplifting the spirits of others with compassion to persevere in life challenges. Assess the quality of your acts of encouragement attribute by inserting an X below the number that best describes your response to each statement.

Item	Acts of Encouragement Attribute Check 1= Always; 2= Frequently; 3= Sometimes; 4= Almost Never; 5= Never	1	2	3	4	5
1	I act enthusiastically in ways that encourage others.					
2	I act in ways that allows me to inspire passion and excitement in people in whatever they are doing.					
3	I act in ways that show that I am more about the people than the project					
4	I do affirm others publicly or privately to inspire or uplift others.					
5	I think and act positively about followers, no matter their productivity					
6	I am consistent, personal, specific, and purposeful in my words of affirmation					
7	I do exalt through praises to honor others for performance and efforts toward a goal.					
8	I do put aside my personal goals to serve others who rely on me					
9	I give service to others to inspire courage, hope or promise,					
10	I act generously with me time and resources to meet the needs of others					
11	**Add up your rating in each column**					
Score Range	Guide and Explanation of Score: understand areas to further develop	Total Score =				
10-17	Great encourager; keep it up					
18-25	Above Average- encourager; need to need to work on 25% of areas;					
26-33:	Average encourager; need to need to work on 50% of the areas					
34-41	Below average encourager; need to need to work on 75% the areas					
42-50:	Not an encourager; need work on all the areas immediately					

CHAPTER 3
DEVELOPING ENCOURAGEMENT-AFFIRMATION

Encouragement-affirmations are declarations given publicly or privately to inspire someone or uplift someone. Affirmation is positioned at the second inner core above enthusiasm because affirmations can be given as often as needed and move toward compassion as shown in Figure 5. A few strategies to consider are discussed in the following sections

BE POSITIVE IN WORDS AND ACTIONS

Affirmation is more likely to come from a leader with a positive and enthusiastic disposition about himself and others than from a negative person. Leaders who think favorably about followers also act positively toward them. They always look for what they can affirm, no matter how small, rather than what they can rebuke from what the followers did wrong or did not do. Such a positive encouragement-affirmation attitude is a very impactful encouragement attribute. The Apostle Paul is known to have such an attribute. He was very intentional in his letters, and his words were purposefully meant to edify and encourage others. Paul wrote:

> *"We are bound to thank God always for you, brethren, as it is fitting, because your faith grows exceedingly, and the love of every one of you all abounds toward each other, so that we ourselves boast of you among the churches of God for your patience and faith in all your persecutions and tribulations that you endure"*
> (2 Thessalonians 1:3-6).

Just notice his careful choice of words—bound to thank God, faith grows, love of everyone, boast of you, your patience, endurance—all designed to encourage them. From the Apostle Paul's letters, the following lessons can be learned about an effective encouragement strategy based on the impact of Paul's words on his followers, even on us in modern times:

BE PERSONAL AND PURPOSEFUL IN WORDS

Be consistent, personal, and purposeful in words. Paul was consistent: "I thank God always;" the use of the word always was to indicate that he took it personally: "we are bound...as it is fitting." Paul never missed a moment to affirm his followers. His encouragement was *purposeful*. Paul's encouragement strategies were to communicate and affirm how much he believed in his brethren, specifically and publicly whenever possible, to let them know what he appreciated in their service. His purpose was to motivate and inspire them. Leaders must readily and often publicly communicate words that show support and encouragement. Privately, they offer wise counsel and guidance in the right direction.

Affirm your followers as a parent affirms and guides a child as was exhorted by Paul: "As ye know how we exhorted and comforted and charged every one of you, as a father doth his children" (1 Thessalonians 2:11). A leader-servant should give his followers affection and warmth. Acts of encouragement are more impacting when they are *specific*. Paul was *specific* as to what he was affirming—their faith and love toward each other; he affirmed believers in public with *reason*—boasted about them among the churches for their patience and faith. Simple words of encouragement like "I love this ___that you did"; I'm proud of you for ____." As Paul noted, it will have the same impact as a father's or mother's affirmation of his or her children. Nurture the followers with good words and spend your time with them. Show support and love through actions as well as words. Being able to identify by name specifically what you are affirming in others has the power of communicating to the person that you are following the person's progress. It also makes the affirmation to be authentic because the person is able to relate. Followers are always able to reciprocate the sentiment of affirmation.

SUMMARY 3
DEVELOPING ENCOURAGEMENT-AFFIRMATION

Before starting this exercise, please read and follow the instruction in the preface of this workbook. Answers to these questions are contained in this chapter. Completion of these exercises after reading the chapter should take 60-90 minutes.

Discovering Acts of Encouragement-Affirmation Leadership Attribute

1. Define Encouragement-affirmation?
2. Being positive in Words and Actions is shown as one such attribute. How did Apostle Paul demonstrate such attribute in (2 Thessalonians 1:3-6).
3. How is being Personal and Purposeful in Words an attribute of encouragement? (1 Thessalonians 2:11).
4. How can a leader make Acts of encouragement more impactful

Practicing Encouragement -Affirmations

1. **As declarations** given publicly or privately for the purpose of inspiring someone or uplifting someone:
    a. Which words do you use to affirm others?
    b. When was the last time you encourage someone by affirmation? What specific affirmative actions did you take? What were the results?
2. With reference to encouragement attribute, what take-away, meaning or lesson can you frame your experience to improve your affirmation of others?

CHAPTER 4
DEVELOPING ENCOURAGEMENT-EXALTATION

Encouragement-exaltation means giving praises publicly or privately for honoring someone for performances and efforts toward a goal. Exaltation is a level of encouragement above affirmation and can be rendered through affirmation but is presented in the form of praise, not just a declaration. Here is a case example:

READINESS TO EXALT FOLLOWERS' PERFORMANCE

Readiness to exalt followers' performance, impact, and potential for greatness is perhaps one of Paul's acts of encouragement to his followers. One of the greatest empowering encouragers in modern times with whom I have ever worked or studied was Dr. Harvey Borovetz, Distinguished Professor and Chair of the Bioengineering Department, at the University of Pittsburgh Swanson School of engineering. What makes Professor Borovetz unique is his ability and readiness to identify the qualities of his followers, affirm, and honor his team, not only in their performance but also in their potential for greatness. He readily, sincerely, and publicly announces specific achievements and their significance to the overall department mission. I have never seen him take the glory even for his own signature achievements, but he is often quick to let the world know about the achievements of his team members. He has a way of connecting with people that does make them feel valued, and they feel they are part of the leadership; furthermore, he readily expresses confidence in his team members. He takes time to express the impact of specific efforts. And, in these days of the Internet, he broadcasts the affirmation publicly, naming the specific achievement he is honoring. Who would not want to work with or follow such a leader like this?

AUTHENTICITY AND CAPACITY TO MOTIVATE

Many elements set Dr. Borovetz, including his authenticity and capacity to motivate his followers through genuine and specific appreciation, affirmation and support for recognition, and inspiration. As a result, his department by all standards is the most productive, with the best climate and the most inclusive culture in which to work. His team follows him and is usually motivated to go the extra mile because he appreciates each team member. When asked what he thought the five characteristics of a good leader should be, he named five empowering leadership qualities:

1. First, he or she must put aside individual/personal goals; leadership is all about the people who rely on you.
2. He empowers those around him or her to achieve the very best successes.
3. He is a good listener, as everyone wants the chance to be at least be heard and, better yet, understood.
4. He treats everyone respectfully and values/appreciate their contributions to the overall mission.
5. He puts himself- or herself in the shoes of persons who are unhappy or who have a disagreement with someone. If, you as a leader were positioned in this way, how would you respond?.

SUMMARY 4
DEVELOPING ENCOURAGEMENT-EXALTATION

Before starting this exercise, please read and follow the instruction in the preface of this workbook. Answers to these questions are contained in this chapter. Completion of these exercises after reading the chapter should take 60-90 minutes.

Discovering the Acts of Encouragement-Affirmations

1. What does Encouragement-exaltation mean? What is the role of exaltation in encouragement?
2. Readiness to Exalt Followers' Performance is an act of affirmation. How this Paul's demonstrate this as an act of encouragement to his followers.

CHAPTER 4
DEVELOPING ENCOURAGEMENT-EXALTATION

    a. How did he empower those around him, like Timothy and Titus to achieve the very best successes?
    b. How did He put himself in the shoes of persons who are unhappy

Practicing the Acts the acts of Encouragement

1. **Encouragement-Exaltations** are praises given publicly or privately for honoring someone for a performance and efforts towards a goal.
    a. How is exaltation as a level of encouragement above affirmation?
    b. List three encouragement-exaltation acts you applied recently to build some up? What was the result?
2. With reference to encouragement attribute, what take-away, meaning or lesson can you frame your experience to improve your exaltation of others?

CHAPTER 5
DEVELOPING ENCOURAGEMENT-COMPASSION

Encouragement-compassion is a leader's acts of compassion that encourage others. An act of compassion is the highest level of encouragement where practical care or service is rendered in serving others, including caring that inspires courage, hope, or promise, and uplifting of the spirit of another person. Typical examples of such acts, as we learned from Barnabas, manifest as generosity to meet needs, courage to stand behind followers in challenging times, kindness, compassion for reconciliation, commitment to mentoring others, and consolation.

BE GENEROUS TO MEET THE NEEDS OF OTHERS

The scripture recorded that Barnabas was a landowner who sold his land and willingly and generously donated the proceeds for the Apostle's upkeep in Jerusalem (Acts 4:36-37). Now imagine the impact that action by today's measure would have had on the Apostle's courage and confidence to continue in the ministry and the impact on their hope in God for providence. If they were fearful as to how they would survive, as is usually the case in such ministries, imagine how they would have felt with Barnabas' gift. They were definitely so encouraged that they agreed to change his name from Joseph to "Son of Encouragement."

BE COURAGEOUS TO STAND BEHIND THE FOLLOWERS

Most courageous leaders are able to stand behind their followers at challenging times. In the very early days of Saul of Tarsus, people in Jerusalem, especially the disciples feared Saul as a persecutor of Christians. Some were casting stones at him. But not Barnabas! He read that several years after he donated the proceeds of selling his land to help the apostles, God appointed Barnabas as an Apostle to the Gentiles, and he was to accompany Saul, now renamed Paul after his conversion (Acts 13:2-3; 14:14). Barnabas remained very courageous to stand by all the messengers in a time of tumult, including believing in Paul's authenticity and standing by him. If you were in Paul's shoes, how would you have felt? Paul definitely felt more confident and more courageous because the encourager "had his back."

POSITIVE ATTITUDE AND COMMITMENT TO MENTOR

Being committed to a mentor with a positive attitude to build up others can be seen as a caring attitude and draws followers to a leader. In the midst of fearing Saul (later Paul), Barnabas was the first person to show a positive attitude toward Paul by extending intimate brotherly warmth and the hand of fellowship at his home (Acts 9:26-31). He extended himself, showed great kindness, and committed himself to mentor Paul to greater prominence, while he remained in a supporting role. Paul gained more clarity in his next course of action because Barnabas showed him the way.

Barnabas was a man who exemplified servant leadership in his commitment to mentor Paul. Barnabas showed the four unique aspects of commitment—dedication, sense of security, self-effacement, and sense of sacrifice—to servant leadership:

- His sense of *dedication to serving*. Barnabas showed dedication to service; by leading, and mentoring others while serving them. Because of Barnabas' contagious humility and witness, others came to believe in the Gospel message.
- His *sense of security*. He showed that he had nothing to lose in serving. Barnabas was people-centered, which enabled him to sell the fields he owned and present the money to the apostles for their use (Acts 4:37). He could rejoice with others' victories (Acts 11:23) and never wondered about his fame.
- His *self-effacement*. When everyone still had reservations about Paul and his conversion, Barnabas showed conviction and belief in Paul's potential and encouraged him and others to remain faithful to the

calling (Acts 11:23). He showed that he had nothing to prove by glorifying his limelight, but instead committed to mentoring Paul, even if it meant Paul rising above him. To Barnabas, this young apostle must grow in his new faith. Barnabas had self-worth and did not see mentoring Paul as a means to prove himself to anyone.

- His *personal sacrifices to grow others*. He nurtured and encouraged other apostles to grow; he inspired the growth of the others; built up, encouraged, and further developed John Mark, who had shown weakness in their earlier missionary trip. Barnabas saw an opportunity to develop John Mark to his fullest potential. John Mark was later confirmed by Peter and Paul when they acknowledged how he had become useful to them.

BRING COMFORT AND RELIEF IN CONSOLATION

Consolation is the act of bringing comfort, hope, or relief to someone in a state of pain, trial, or suffering. The word "encouragement" has been translated by scholars as consolation, comfort, and exhortation (Acts 4:36), all of which can be seen as characteristics of encouragement. Some believers had scattered due to the persecution that broke out when Stephen was killed and some traveled as far as Phoenicia, Cyprus, and Antioch, spreading the word only among Jews (Acts 11:20). Many believers were added. When the news reached the church in Jerusalem, they sent Barnabas to Antioch.

Bring hope to others. The reason Barnabas was sent can be debated. There is no debate that he was a man who set himself apart as an encourager. One possible reason for sending him was because he was the most likely to bring comfort and hope to the disciples amidst the mix of progress and pain due to the death of Stephen. Barnabas came onto the scene immediately and during the turmoil. Barnabas was a minister sent "to establish and encourage the believers concerning their faith" (I Thessalonians 3:2-3), as Luke described him as a good man of faith.

Share in others' suffering to comfort. Consolation is an important element of encouragement because of the continued trials and sufferings of those under us. To encourage people under some suffering is like sharing the suffering of Christ. The Bible shows that it involves comforting others drawing on the comfort and consolation we received from God. Barnabas was to help the Christians in Antioch triumph over their trials, even as they made more progress. And, we see that he did just that, bring them together first in fellowship as Christians. Paul wrote about this when he said, "Now may our Lord Jesus Christ Himself, and our God and Father, who has loved us and given us everlasting consolation and good hope by grace, comfort your hearts and establish you in every good word and work" (II Thessalonians 2:16-17).

ENGAGE IN RECONCILIATION TO BUILD RELATIONSHIPS

Engage in conflict management as an act of compassion and reconciliation. As new relationships formed after Christ's resurrection, especially among fresh converts, with new and exploratory teaching, and with little to guide their leadership except what they learned from Christ and the Holy Spirit, disagreements were inevitable. Conflict resolution, however, is part of the leadership process. Barnabas and Paul experienced a period of conflict, possibly tensions over John Mark, who was Barnabas' cousin (Acts 15:36-41). John Mark's decision in Pamphylia to leave them and their work created the conflict and resulted in Paul and Barnabas heading separate ways—Barnabas moved on with John Mark to Cyprus, and Paul chose to continue with Silas to Syria and Cilicia. Nevertheless, all of them focused on the same mission agenda. Paul and Barnabas later reconciled and talked about supporting the work of God and the ministry to which they were called and which they saw as much bigger than both of them combined (1 Corinthians 9:6).

In summary, Barnabas was kind and generous in his acts of service; he demonstrated a positive attitude to forgive and reconcile with Paul. Luke summarized it this way: "When he came and had seen the grace of God, he was glad and encouraged them all that with the purpose of heart they should continue with the Lord" (Acts 11:23, NKJV) Luke further portrayed the character of Barnabas as "A good man, full of the Holy Spirit and of faith" (Acts 11:24) and that "a great many people were added to the Lord" (Acts 11:24b).

Barnabas' acts of encouragement were instrumental in the first gathering of believers in Antioch and they are being named Christians:

CHAPTER 5
DEVELOPING ENCOURAGEMENT–COMPASSION

"And when he had found him (Saul), he brought him to Antioch. So it was that for a whole year, they assembled with the church and taught a great many people. And the disciples were first called Christians in Antioch" (Acts 11:26). His acts of kindness and generosity and his forgiving nature helped pull the disciples together, consoled them in the death of Stephen, and encouraged them with a course of action. All the members in Antioch he "encouraged… that with a purpose of heart, they should continue with the Lord" (Acts 11:23). In the words of the Apostle Paul, Barnabas consoled the believers in Antioch with the knowledge that "as the sufferings of Christ abound in us, so our consolation also abounds through Christ" (II Corinthians 1:5).

SUMMARY 5
DEVELOPING ENCOURAGEMENT–COMPASSION

Before starting this exercise, please read and follow the instruction in the preface of this workbook. Answers to these questions are contained in this chapter. Completion of these exercises after reading the chapter should take 60-90 minutes

Discovering the Acts of Encouragement-Compassion

1. What is Encouragement-compassion? Why is an act of compassion the highest level of encouragement? Give some examples of such acts.
2. Why and how is compassion the highest level of the encouragement act?
3. How can practical care or service rendered in serving others be an act of compassion?
4. What was the impact of Barnabas' acts of encouragement (Acts 11:23-26)? How did Barnabas console the believers in Antioch (II Corinthians 1:5)?
5. Being Generous to Meet the Needs of Others is an act of compassion. How Barnabas demonstrate this act? (<u>Acts 4:36</u>-37)?
6. How can you be Courageous to Stand Behind the Followers?

Practicing the Acts of Encouragement-Compassion

1. Being committed to a mentor with a positive attitude to build up others can be seen as a caring attitude and draws followers to a

leader. How did Barnabas demonstrate this act in his service and work with Paul (Acts 9:26-31) and what was the outcome?
2. In what four ways did Barnabas exemplify servant leadership in his commitment to mentor Paul. (Acts 4:37 (Acts 11:23)?
3. Consolation is the act of bringing comfort, hope, or relief to someone in a state of pain, trial, or suffering. In what ways did Barnabas demonstrate this as a minister sent "to establish and encourage the believers concerning their faith" (I Thessalonians 3:2-3), as Luke described him as a good man of faith. (II Thessalonians 2:16-17).?
4. Engaging in conflict management is an act of compassion and reconciliation. How was this handled in working relationship between Barnabas and Paul (Acts 15:36-41);(1 Corinthians 9:6). What was the outcome?
5. How did Barnabas demonstrate kindness, generosity and positive attitude to forgive and reconcile with Paul? (Acts 11:23, NKJV) How did Luke portray the character of Barnabas in (Acts 11:24) and what was the outcome (Acts 11:24b)?
6. With reference to encouragement attribute, what take-away, meaning or lesson can you frame your experience to improve your acts of compassion toward others?

Topic Index

About This Book, 22
AFFECTIVE COMPASSION, 67
authentic, 24, 26
authentic leadership, 37
Authentic Leadership, 45
Authenticity, 43
Comfort, 41
commitment, 19, 25
communication
    types of, 30
Communication, 30
Comparisons
    with other works, 40
Compassion, 28
credibility, 48
Empathy-attribute, 28
encouragement
    definition, 53, 54, 57, 58
Encouragement- affirmation, 59, 61
Encouragement-compassion, 67, 71
Encouragement-enthusiasm, 55, 57, 58
Encouragement-exaltation, 58, 63, 64, 65
Functional Definitions, 35
giving, 58, 61, 63, 65
Initiative
    definition of, 29
inside-out, 46
Joshua, 19
law of, 42
LEADER, 28

Leader as Servant Leadership, 42
    definition, 25
Leader First., 23
Leader-as-Servant Leadership, 23
leader-servant's affection-attribute
    definition, 48
leadership, 25
Leadership Attributes, 43
Leadership Inner Value system, 25
Model, 23
Moses, 19
Navigation-attribute, 48
Personal Outward Authenticity, 47
Practicing Servant Leadership
    Encouragement, 57
process, 25
Reconciliation, 67, 70
Servant, 23, 24
suffering, 56
Teachable Moments to Grow, 72
test
    for leader-servant authenticity, 46
    of essential elements of personal authenticity, 46, 47
The Leadership Influence-attribute, 41
The Principle of Leadership Empathy-Attribute, 28
The Principle of Leadership Adaptability Attribute, 27
The Principle of Leadership listening-attribute, 30

REFERENCES

[1] Greenleaf, R. (1970). *The Servant as Leader,* Indianapolis: The Robert K. Greenleaf Center

[2] Spears, L. (1996). *"Reflections on Robert K. Greenleaf and servant-leadership."* Leadership & Organization Development Journal, 17(7), 33-35

[3] Russell, R.F. (2001). "The role of values in servant leadership." *Leadership & Organization Development Journal,* 22(2), 76-83

[4] Russell, R.F., and Stone, A.G. (2002). "A review of servant leadership attributes: developing a practical model." *Leadership & Organization Development Journal,* 23(3), 145-15

[5] Terry. R. W (1993). *Authentic Leadership: Courage In Action*, San Francisco, CA, Jossey-Bass

[6] George, B (2003). *Authentic Leadership: Rediscovering the Secrets to Creating Lasting Value.* San Francisco, CA, Jossey-Bass

[7] Shamir, B. & Eilam, G. (2005). "What's your story? Toward a life-story approach to authentic leadership." Leadership Quarterly, 16, 395–418.

[8] Anderson, GL (2009). *Advocacy Leadership: Toward a Post-Reform Agenda in Education*, Routledge, New York, 41

[9] Yacobi, B.G. *"Elements of Human Authenticity."* http://www.philosophytogo.org /wordpress/?p=1945, Retrieved, July 15, 2012

[10] George, B (2003). *Authentic Leadership: Rediscovering the Secrets to Creating Lasting Value*, San Francisco, CA, Jossey-Bass

[11] Wosu, SN (2014), *Leader as Servant Leadership Model,* Xulon Press

[12] Heaphy, E.D. & J.E. Dutton (2004) 'Embodied connections: Understanding the physiological effects of positive connections at work.' Working paper, Center for Positive Organizational Scholarship, University of Michigan Business School.

[13] US. Department of labor. "Mastering Soft Skills for Workplace Success", Washington DC

www.ingramcontent.com/pod-product-compliance
Lightning Source LLC
LaVergne TN
LVHW061600070526
838199LV00077B/7123